Adult supervision is recommended to make the recipes in this book. Adults should handle anything that requires cooking over heat or with an oven. Check with an adult to make sure you don't have allergies or sensitivities to any of the ingredients used in these recipes. All tips are for entertainment only, and any diet changes should be discussed with a doctor.

Any website addresses listed in the book are correct at the time of going to print. However, please be aware that online content is subject to change and websites can contain or offer content that is unsuitable for children. We advise all children be supervised when using the internet.

BuzzPop

An imprint of Little Bee Books
New York, NY
Text copyright © 2020 by Omari McQueen
Photography © 2020 by Scholastic Children's Books
Recipe Testing, Prop Styling and Editorial: Nicola Graimes
Omari and Family Photography: Haarala Hamilton Photography
Ingredient Photography: Silvio Bukbardis
Food Photography: Xavier D. Buendi
Shutterstock: 51, 55, 63, 64, 71 vegetable stock margouillat photo;
75 lime wedges Deviatov Aleksei; 98 Animal Crackers jeehyun;
100 graham crackers Dunetrune Studios
Senior Designer: Aimee Stewart
First published in the UK by Scholastic Children's Books.
This BuzzPop edition, 2022.
All rights reserved, including the right of reproduction in whole or in part in any form.
Manufactured in China   RRD 0122

Library of Congress Catologing-in-Publication is available upon request.
ISBN 978-1-4998-1261-9 (hardcover)
First Edition 2 4 6 8 10 9 7 5 3 1
ISBN 978-1-49981262-6 (ebook)
buzzpopbooks.com

For information about special discounts on bulk purchases,
please contact Little Bee Books at sales@littlebeebooks.com.

OMARI McQUEEN'S BEST BITES COOKBOOK

BuzzPop

CONTENTS

HI, I'M OMARI McQUEEN!

**I'm an everyday boy from south London
with a huge passion for vegan cooking.**

It all started when I was eight years old and began making vegan dips in my kitchen at home. I started my own business, Dipalicious, and started to sell my dips at fairs and events. Then I opened my first pop-up restaurant in August 2019, and the rest is history!

I've worked with lots of well-known companies and have also cooked on television programs. I am now a multi-award-winning vegan chef, and—guess what?—I'm the youngest vegan chef in the UK and one of the youngest restauranteurs in the world. Plus, I have my own TV show!

**I wanted to write this book for you and your family, as
I love bringing people together through food, without
harming animals.**

This book is full of fun and delicious vegan recipes with a taste of the Caribbean, since my family is from Jamaica and Antigua. I've learnt how to mix lots of different flavors and ingredients to merge different cultures. My dad was the first person to teach me how to cook when my mom got really ill and could no longer cook safely in the kitchen. At first, it was just helping out getting things he needed—the usual things adults give us kids to do! Then my dad started to allow me to experiment in the kitchen as I really wanted to cook by myself.

**So, now it's your turn to experiment in the kitchen and
to cook meals that will blow your parents' minds.**

LET'S GET COOKING!

WHAT DOES IT MEAN TO BE VEGAN?

To me, being vegan means that you avoid all animal products for ethical, health, or environmental reasons. A vegan does not use, eat, or wear any products that are related to animals. Some people think that veganism is a diet, but it's not just that—it's a way of life!

Vegans like myself eat tasty plant-based foods instead of meat, fish, eggs, or dairy. But it doesn't end there. This may come as a surprise to you, but vegans don't eat honey (because it comes from bees) and they don't use products like palm oil because deforestation to produce palm oil affects natural habitats.

Vegans do not use any products that have been tested on animals or wear clothing or shoes made from animal products, such as leather or snakeskin. But don't worry, being vegan doesn't mean that you have to walk around with bare feet and no clothes on—there are many vegan alternatives to these materials!

BE MORE VEGAN: OMARI'S TOP TIPS

1. Write down a menu for the week's meals. It helps to make a shopping list with everything you need for the coming week.

2. Get ahead. Some meals can be made in advance and chilled or frozen.

3. Write down your favorite meals and look for their vegan alternatives. There are lots of great vegan egg, dairy, and meat replacements available in grocery stores.

4. Check out the benefits—health, animal, and environmental—of the vegan foods available.

5. Read all food labels and double check that the products are vegan.

6. Try different types of fruits and vegetables—even the funny-looking ones! Remember that trying new foods is all part of experimenting with your taste buds.

7. The kitchen is like a science lab and it's fun to experiment with new flavors! Try out different seasonings and spices. Check the label first before buying, as some herb and spice mixes, such as all-purpose seasoning, can contain additives or extra salt.

8. I love to use big flavors like hot chili peppers in my vegan cooking, but if you're new to cooking with herbs, spices, and chili peppers you can start off using smaller amounts and then build up the flavors.

OMARI'S ESSENTIAL INGREDIENTS

You may never have heard of some of my most-used ingredients before. Here's some more information to help you learn about what they are, and where you can find them!

ACKEE
The national fruit of Jamaica, which is used as a vegetable! Ackee has a creamy texture and mild taste and can be bought in cans in supermarkets and world food markets.

ALL-PURPOSE SEASONING
This is a mixture of herbs, spices, and salt. It can include smoked paprika, onion powder, garlic powder, coriander, chili powder, celery powder, cayenne pepper, and ground cumin. You can buy it in a store, or even make your own! Always be careful of how much salt you put into your cooking.

BANANA
Look for bananas that are bright yellow in color—this is a sign they are ripe and taste sweet. Unripe green bananas are also popular in Caribbean cooking in savory dishes.

BEANS & LEGUMES (CHICKPEAS, BUTTER BEANS, KIDNEY BEANS—AND LENTILS)
Beans are great for vegans as they are a good source of protein. They are also used a lot in Caribbean cooking. I like chickpeas, butter beans, and kidney beans (and lentils!). Confusingly, red kidney beans are called "peas" when cooked in the traditional dish, Rice 'n' Peas (see page 82).

CALLALOO

A popular green leafy vegetable in the Caribbean that you can buy fresh or in cans. I use canned in this book as it is easy to use—if you can't find it in supermarkets or international food markets, spinach is a great alternative.

COCONUT

Coconut palms have grown in the Caribbean for thousands of years. The sweet, creamy flesh of the fruit is used in sweet and savory cooking. I use the milk, cream, oil, and grated coconut in my recipes.

GINGER

This root is grated and often used as a spice to flavor food. It has a bit of heat to it and can be used in sweet and savory food.

JACKFRUIT

This is a meat substitute in vegan cooking. Sold fresh and raw in cans, it has quite a mild, fruity flavor that loves spices—jerk jackfruit is the best!

JERK SEASONING & JERK MARINADE

You can make jerk seasoning at home or buy it, too. It is usually a blend of cinnamon, thyme, allspice, nutmeg, black pepper, and Scotch bonnet pepper. Jerk marinade is a sauce with a similar great taste that you can use in your cooking. Beware, it can be hot!

HEART OF PALM

This delicious, crunchy vegetable comes from the middle of a type of palm tree. The vegetable is cut into cylinders and looks like a smooth, white stalk. Buy it in cans from supermarkets and international food markets.

LIME

A squeeze of this bright green citrus fruit is the best on just about everything—sweet or savory. Like lemons, limes are high in vitamin C.

MANGO

Sweet and juicy, what's not to like about mango! This is just one of my favorite tropical fruits—I'd also add pineapple, passion fruit, and papaya to the list, too.

PAPRIKA

This spice is made from ground sweet red peppers and gives food a great color. Even though it looks like chili powder, it isn't hot in flavor. You can also buy smoked paprika, which has a stronger taste and comes in mild and hot.

YAM

This vegetable tastes a bit like potatoes, and you can use it in the same way—mash or boil it, fry or bake as fries and tots. It comes in different shapes and colors, but I usually use the type with a tough brown outer skin and cream or white center. Look for it in international food markets.

RICE
At the heart of Caribbean food is a good bowl of rice, especially the classic Rice 'n' Peas. I use basmati rice in this book—both brown and white.

SCOTCH BONNET PEPPER
I love spicy food, and the Scotch bonnet is very hot! To make the pepper less spicy use it whole and add to a dish halfway through cooking, or you can remove the seeds—but make sure you wear gloves! If you can't find any Scotch bonnets at your local store, you can substitue habanero peppers.

GREEN ONIONS
These have a milder taste than regular onions and are used to add flavor and color to many Caribbean dishes. They are also called scallions.

SWEET POTATO
They come in cream, purple, and yellow varieties, but my go-to sweet potato is orange inside. Baked whole, added to stews, or mashed—I love it!

TURMERIC
This spice adds a bright yellow color to stews, curries, and patties. It's also really good for you!

THYME
I like to use this herb fresh and dried in lots of different dishes, from jerk seasoning and curries to stews and bakes.

LIGHT BITES!

MILD

WHAT YOU NEED:

15 ounce can chickpeas,
liquid reserved

1 tablespoon extra-virgin
olive oil, plus extra to serve

3 tablespoons tahini

Juice of 1 small lemon

1 garlic clove, peeled

salt & black pepper

all-purpose seasoning,
for sprinkling

HAPPY HUMMUS

Serves 4-6
Takes 10 minutes

This tasty hummus is so easy to make and is
dipalicious scooped up on some toasted pita bread or
vegetable sticks.

1 Drain the chickpeas (saving the liquid from the can) and tip
them into a food processor or blender.

2 Add the olive oil, tahini, lemon juice, garlic, and a good pinch
of salt and pepper, then blend until smooth and creamy. If the
hummus is too thick to blend, add some of the saved liquid
from the drained can of chickpeas—I used about 4 tablespoons.

3 Spoon the hummus into a bowl and drizzle over a little extra
olive oil. Add a sprinkle of all-purpose seasoning, if you like.
Now chow down! Dunk vegetable sticks and pita bread into the
hummus.

TAKE CARE...
Always ask an adult for help when using a sharp knife or
peeler, kitchen appliances, and the hot oven.

DID YOU KNOW?

Chickpeas have been used in cooking since ancient times by the Egyptians, Greeks, and Romans.

DID YOU KNOW?

Tomatoes are a fruit, not a vegetable, as they contain seeds—even though they are used as a vegetable!

MEDIUM

WHAT YOU NEED:

1 tablespoon extra-virgin
olive oil, plus extra to serve

1 onion, finely chopped

1 large garlic clove,
finely chopped

2 red jalapeño chilis, deseeded
and finely chopped (optional)

15 ounce can
chopped tomatoes

½–1 tsp all-purpose
seasoning, or to taste

Juice of ½ lime

Handful of fresh cilantro
leaves, chopped

salt & black pepper

SALSA TIME

Serves 4-6
Takes 20 minutes

This tomato dip contains a tasty blend of herbs, spices, and
chili pepper. It can be hot so be careful if you don't like spice.
Personally, I love it! Dunk in tortilla chips for a delicious snack.

1 Heat the oil in a saucepan over medium heat. Add the finely
chopped onion and cook, stirring occasionally, for 6 minutes
until softened. Add the finely chopped garlic and jalapeño
chili, if using, and cook for another minute, stirring.

2 Pour in the chopped tomatoes and all-purpose seasoning—
add the smaller amount if you prefer it mild or add more if
you like things hot—and simmer over a low heat for 5 minutes,
stirring occasionally, until reduced and thickened
a little.

3 Spoon the salsa into a bowl (or you can blend it if you like
a smooth salsa) and stir in the lime juice and cilantro leaves.
Season with salt and pepper to taste. Spoon into a serving
bowl and serve with tortilla chips.

Take care...
Only use the jalapeño chilis if you like heat—it's spicy! It's a good
idea to wear rubber gloves when chopping up pepper, and make
sure you don't touch your face after cutting it.

MILD

WHAT YOU NEED:

15 ounce can
butter beans,
drained and
rinsed

3 ½ tablespoons
vegan butter

1 garlic clove,
crushed

1–2 red jalapeño chilis,
deseeded and finely
chopped (optional)

4 tablespoons
nutritional yeast flakes

1 teaspoon
onion powder

⅓ cup
oat milk

1 teaspoon
smoked paprika

1 teaspoon
ground cumin

½–1 teaspoon
dried chili flakes
(optional)

1 teaspoon
lemon juice

salt &
black pepper

NICELY CHEESY DIP

Serves 4-6
Takes 20 minutes

You won't believe this dip doesn't contain cheese! I like to top it with freshly chopped tomatoes and dunk in tortilla chips.

1 Put the drained and rinsed butter beans in a saucepan with the vegan butter, garlic, and jalapeño chili, if using, and warm gently over medium-low heat until the butter melts. Stir the mixture occasionally.

2 Add the nutritional yeast flakes, onion powder, oat milk, smoked paprika, cumin, and dried chili flakes, if using, and cook over medium-low heat for 5 minutes, stirring, until reduced and thickened slightly.

3 Tip the bean mixture into a blender or use an electric hand blender. Add the lemon juice and blend until smooth and creamy. It should be like a thick sauce—add another tablespoon of oat milk if it is too thick to blend.

4 Spoon the dip into a bowl and season with salt and pepper to taste. It is best served warm.

DID YOU KNOW?

Oat milk tastes rich and creamy and is a great alternative to dairy milk from cows. It's also delicious poured over breakfast cereal in the morning.

NO SPICE

WHAT YOU NEED:

1 banana, peeled and
cut into chunks

½ mango, peeled,
pit removed, and diced

1 passion fruit,
cut in half

1 ¼ cups tropical fruit juice

RISING SUN FRUIT PUNCH

Serves 2
Takes 10 minutes, plus freezing

Refreshing and fruity, this is delicious served chilled on a hot day! Freezing the banana first makes it extra creamy and super-chilled, but you don't have to do this if you're in a hurry.

1 Put the banana chunks on a baking tray and freeze for about 1 hour until firmed up (this is optional).

2 Peel the mango using a vegetable peeler, then cut away the fruit around the large pit in the middle.

3 Scoop out the passion fruit with a spoon.

4 Put the banana, mango, passion fruit, and tropical juice in a blender and blend until smooth—there may be a few seedy bits so strain it through a sieve if you prefer. Pour into two glasses and enjoy!

NO SPICE

WHAT YOU NEED:

2 bananas, peeled and cut into chunks

½ cup blackberries

1 ¼ cups coconut drinking milk

½ cup strawberries, hulled

1 tablespoon maple syrup

MOMMA BEAR SMOOTHIE

Serves 2
Takes 5 minutes, plus freezing

If it's a hot day, I like to put the ingredients for this fruit smoothie in the freezer first, just so everything is nice and chilled.

1 Put the banana chunks, blackberries, and strawberries on a baking tray and freeze for about 1 hour until firmed up (this is optional).

2 Take the fruit out of the freezer and place in a blender with the rest of the ingredients. Blend everything until smooth and creamy. Pour into two glasses, and add straws.

DID YOU KNOW?

Coconut is the fruit (even though it's called a nut!) of the coconut palm, which is known as the "tree of life."

NO SPICE

WHAT YOU NEED:

1 large banana, peeled and cut into chunks

½ cup canned or fresh pineapple pieces

2 teaspoons hulled hemp seeds

1 large handful baby spinach leaves, stalks removed

1 ¼ cups coconut drinking milk

GO-GO ENERGY SMOOTHIE

Serves 2
Takes 5 minutes, plus freezing

This smoothie contains spinach, though you really wouldn't know it! It makes for a great energy-boosting start to the day.

1 Put the banana chunks and pineapple on a baking tray and freeze for about 1 hour until firmed up (this is optional).

2 Take the banana and pineapple out of the freezer and place in a blender with the rest of the ingredients. Blend everything until smooth and creamy. Pour into two glasses, add straws, and drink right away while it's still cool.

LUNCH TIME!

· ·

MILD

WHAT YOU NEED:

1 tablespoon olive oil

2 large leeks, sliced

2 garlic cloves, chopped

3 white potatoes, about
1 ¼ lbs, peeled and chopped

1 teaspoon mild curry powder

1 teaspoon
all-purpose seasoning

½ teaspoon turmeric powder

1 vegetable stock cube

¾ cup and 1 tablespoon
oat milk

salt & black pepper

LEEK & POTATO SOUP

Serves 4
Takes 25 minutes

This popular vegetable soup has been given a spicy twist with the addition of mild curry powder and turmeric. If spices aren't your thing you can leave them out.

1 Bring 4 ¼ cups of water to a boil. Crumble the vegetable stock cube into the water, stir until dissolved, and set aside.

2 Heat the olive oil in a large saucepan over medium heat. Stir in the sliced leeks and cook, stirring often, for 5 minutes until nice and soft.

3 Add the chopped garlic, chopped potatoes, curry powder, all-purpose seasoning, and turmeric and give it a good stir.

4 Pour prepared vegetable stock into the pan and bring to a boil, then turn the heat down low. Partially cover the pan with a lid and simmer for 10 minutes or until the potatoes are soft.

5 Pour in the oat milk and warm through briefly.

6 Blend using an electric hand blender until smooth and creamy. Season with salt and pepper to taste. Now it's time to serve the soup with roti or your favorite bread.

DID YOU KNOW?

Turmeric has been used for centuries in traditional Indian medicine for its anti-inflammatory properties thanks to an ingredient called curcumin.

SPICE ALERT!

JAMAICAN PATTIES

Serves 6
Takes 1 hour, 30 minutes, plus chilling

This vegan version of the famous Jamaican patty is delicious—who needs meat!

WHAT YOU NEED:

For the pastry:

2 cups all-purpose flour   1 ½ tablespoons turmeric powder

1 teaspoon curry powder   ½ teaspoon salt

8 ½ tablespoons vegan butter, cut into small pieces, chilled

For the filling:

1 tablespoon olive oil   4 green onions, chopped

3 garlic cloves, finely chopped   6 ½ ounces chilled or frozen vegan ground "beef"

½ Scotch bonnet pepper, deseeded and finely chopped (optional)   ½ teaspoon ground allspice

1 teaspoon ground cumin   1 teaspoon dried thyme

2 tablespoons coconut milk   2 tablespoons tomato paste

1 teaspoon jerk marinade   ½ cup frozen peas

½ cup canned sweetcorn   3 tablespoons vegan butter, melted

salt & black pepper

1 To make the pastry, mix together the flour, turmeric, curry powder, and salt in a large mixing bowl. Using your fingertips, rub the vegan butter into the flour mixture until it looks like breadcrumbs. Gradually stir in about 3 tablespoons ice-cold water using a fork and then your fingers until the mixture comes together into a ball of dough. Wrap in plastic wrap and chill for 30 minutes.

2 Meanwhile, heat the olive oil in a large frying pan over medium heat. Add the chopped green onions and finely chopped garlic and cook, stirring occasionally, for 1 minute until soft. Add the ground "beef," Scotch bonnet pepper, ground allspice, cumin, and thyme and cook for 5 minutes, stirring to break up the "beef."

3 Add the coconut milk, tomato paste, and jerk marinade, then stir in the peas and sweetcorn and cook for 5 minutes until the peas are tender. Season with salt and pepper and carefully pour the mixture into a bowl and leave to cool.

4 Preheat the oven to 350°F. Line a large baking tray with parchment paper.

5 To make the patties, unwrap the pastry and divide into 6 equally sized pieces. Roll out one of the pieces on a lightly floured work surface into a 6 inch diameter circle, about ¼ inch thick. Wet the rim of the pastry with a finger dipped in water. Place 2 heaped tablespoons of the filling mixture on the bottom half of the pastry, near the middle. Fold the pastry over the filling into a half-moon shape. Use a fork to seal the edges and prick the top 3 times.

6 Place the patty on the lined baking tray and repeat to make 6 in total. Brush the tops of the patties with melted butter and bake for 35 minutes until the pastry is cooked and golden. Leave to cool a little, then eat up!

WHAT YOU NEED:

3 tablespoons
olive oil

1 onion,
chopped

2 carrots, peeled
and diced

1 red pepper,
deseeded and chopped

1–2 garlic
cloves, crushed

½ teaspoon
thyme

1 tomato,
chopped

19 ounce can callaloo,
drained and rinsed

3 ⅓ cups
baby spinach
leaves

½ teaspoon
paprika

1 teaspoon
all-purpose seasoning

1 Scotch bonnet
pepper
(leave whole)
(optional)

salt & black pepper

CALLALOO MIX-UP

Serves 4
Takes 35 minutes

Callaloo is a healthy leafy green vegetable, a bit like spinach, and is also the name of a popular dish in Caribbean cooking. My version is a bit like a Jamaican stir-fry!

1 Heat the oil in a large, deep frying pan with a lid over medium heat. Add the chopped onion and cook, stirring often, for 5 minutes until softened.

2 Add the diced carrots and chopped red pepper and cook, stirring often, for 5 minutes until softened.

3 Next, add the garlic, thyme, tomato, callaloo, spinach, paprika, all-purpose seasoning, Scotch bonnet pepper, if using, and 2 tablespoons water. Turn the heat down a little and cover the pan with a lid. Cook, stirring occasionally, for 7–10 minutes until the vegetables are tender. Add a splash more water if it looks too dry. Season with salt and pepper to taste.

4 Now is the time to serve the callaloo—you can eat it with bread, rice, fried dumplings, or Jamaican boiled hard food (dumpling, banana, and yam). It also makes a great side dish!

Take care...

Only use the Scotch bonnet pepper if you like lots of heat—it's very spicy! You could use a milder tasting pepper instead, like a jalapeño, or leave it out altogether. It's a good idea to wear rubber gloves when chopping up pepper, and make sure you don't touch your face after cutting it.

 **MEDIUM**

WHAT YOU NEED:

2 sweet potatoes, about a pound

2 tablespoons sunflower oil, plus extra for frying

1 small red onion, finely chopped

2 green onions, thinly sliced

2 garlic cloves, chopped

1 teaspoon jerk marinade

1 teaspoon all-purpose seasoning

15 ounce can chickpeas, drained

salt & black pepper

Flour, for coating your hands

⅔ cup breadcrumbs

SWEET POTATO & CHICKPEA BURGERS

Serves 4
Takes 30 minutes, plus chilling

These spicy burgers are the best—serve in a bun with your favorite sauces, relishes, and toppings.

1 Microwave the sweet potatoes on medium high for 6 minutes or until tender when pierced with a fork (or bake them at 400°F for 50 minutes).

2 Meanwhile, heat the oil in a large frying pan over medium heat. Add the finely chopped red onion and thinly sliced green onions and cook, stirring often, for 5 minutes until softened.

3 Add the chopped garlic, jerk marinade, and all-purpose seasoning and cook for another minute. Spoon the mixture into a large bowl and leave to cool.

4 Pour the chickpeas into a bowl and mash with the back of a fork to a crumbly mixture.

5 When the sweet potato is ready, cut each one in half and scoop out the middle with a spoon. Roughly mash the sweet potato and pour into the bowl with the fried onion mixture. Stir in the mashed chickpeas until everything is mixed together and season with salt and pepper to taste. Leave to cool.

6 Pour the breadcrumbs onto a plate.

7 Coat your hands with flour and shape the sweet potato mixture into 4 patties. Dunk them into the breadcrumbs until coated on both sides. Place on a plate and chill for 30 minutes to firm up.

8 Pour enough oil to generously coat the bottom of a large frying pan over medium heat. Cook the patties for 5 minutes on each side until golden and crisp. Serve in a burger bun with all your favorite extras!

MILD

WHAT YOU NEED:

1 tablespoon
olive oil

1 onion,
finely chopped

2 garlic cloves,
finely chopped

¼ inch piece fresh
ginger, peeled and
finely chopped

1–2 teaspoons
garam masala

¼–½ teaspoon
mild chili powder
(optional)

1 potato, about
¼ pound, peeled
and diced

1 carrot, peeled
and diced

6 ½ ounces
chilled or frozen
vegan ground "beef"

2 tablespoons
tomato paste

¾ cup
frozen peas

salt & black
pepper

4 soft flour
tortillas, to serve

1 handful of grated
vegan cheese

SPICY VEGETABLE WRAPS

Serves 4
Takes 40 minutes

I've given these wraps a mild spice rating, but it is virtually medium so take it easy if you don't like spice! Top the wrap with shredded lettuce, if you like.

1 Heat the oil in a large frying pan with a lid over medium heat. Add the finely chopped onion and cook, stirring often, for 5 minutes until softened.

2 Add the finely chopped garlic and ginger and cook, stirring, for another minute.

3 Stir in the garam masala, chili powder, if using, the potato, diced carrot, vegan ground "beef," tomato paste and ⅔ cup of water. Stir well, breaking up the ground "beef" with the back of a fork. When the mixture starts to bubble, turn the heat to low and cover with a lid. Simmer, stirring occasionally, for 10–15 minutes until the potato and carrot are tender.

4 Add the frozen peas and cook for 3 minutes until tender. Taste and season with salt and pepper, if needed.

5 Meanwhile, wrap the tortillas in foil and warm on low heat in an oven.

6 Spoon the "beef" mixture onto each tortilla. Top with the grated vegan cheese (you could also add some shredded lettuce). Serve the tortillas open or rolled up, tucking in the ends, then cut in half before serving. Enjoy!

DID YOU KNOW?
Ginger may help to fight germs in the body and is good for our digestive systems.

DID YOU KNOW?

Ackee is the national fruit of Jamaica. It makes a great vegan scrambled egg!

WHAT YOU NEED:

15 ounce can hearts of palm, drained and shredded

1 tablespoon vegan fish seasoning or light soy sauce

2 tablespoons olive oil

1 onion, chopped

2 peppers (green and red), deseeded and chopped

2 garlic cloves, finely chopped

1 Scotch bonnet pepper, left whole, or 1 jalapeño pepper, deseeded and chopped (optional)

2 green onions, chopped

5 tomatoes, chopped

1 teaspoon all-purpose seasoning

2 teaspoons fresh thyme leaves

19 ounce can ackee, drained

salt & black pepper

1 handful of parsley leaves, chopped

ACKEE & HEARTS OF PALM

Serves 4
Takes 40 minutes

This is my vegan version of the traditional Caribbean dish of ackee and salt fish—I think it's just as good!

1 Put the hearts of palm in a bowl and pull apart into long strips. Pour over the fish sauce, turn until coated, and leave to marinate while you prepare the rest of the dish.

2 Meanwhile, heat the oil in a large, deep frying pan over medium heat. Add the chopped onion and cook, stirring occasionally, for 5 minutes, until softened.

3 Add the chopped green and red peppers and cook for another 5 minutes until tender.

4 Add the garlic, Scotch bonnet pepper, if using, green onions, tomatoes, all-purpose seasoning, and thyme and cook for another 2 minutes until softened.

5 Add the ackee and hearts of palm with the vegan fish sauce and stir gently until combined. Season with salt and pepper and heat through, stirring. Take out the Scotch bonnet pepper. Spoon onto a serving plate and scatter with the parsley—enjoy your lunch!

Take care...

Only use the Scotch bonnet pepper if you like lots of heat—it's very spicy! You could use a milder tasting pepper instead, like a jalapeño, or leave it out altogether. It's a good idea to wear rubber gloves when chopping up pepper, and make sure you don't touch your face after cutting it.

WHAT YOU NEED:

15 ounce can
jackfruit, drained

1 tablespoon
olive oil

1 onion,
chopped

2 garlic cloves,
crushed

1 teaspoon
dried thyme

1 teaspoon
all-purpose
seasoning

1 teaspoon
jerk marinade

4 tablespoons of
your favorite
barbecue sauce

2 teaspoons
white wine
vinegar

6 ounce can
chopped
tomatoes

salt & black pepper

BBQ JACKFRUIT

Serves 4
Takes 1 hour

Jackfruit makes a great vegan alternative to meat. Look for it in cans packed in water, not syrup, for this recipe. Some say it tastes just like pulled pork when cooked in a barbecue sauce!

1 Remove the seeds from the canned jackfruit and cut any large pieces in half.

2 Heat the oil in saucepan over medium heat. Add the chopped onion and cook, stirring often, for 5 minutes until softened. Add the crushed garlic and cook for another minute.

3 Add the thyme, all-purpose seasoning, and jerk marinade. Stir, then add the jackfruit, barbecue sauce, vinegar, chopped tomatoes, and ⅔ cup water. When the sauce starts to bubble turn the heat to low, cover with a lid, and simmer for 30 minutes. Stir the sauce every now and then to stop it sticking to the bottom of the pan.

4 Take the lid off and cook for another 5 minutes until the sauce has reduced and thickened.

5 Preheat the oven to 425°F. Line a large baking tray with parchment paper.

6 Spoon the jackfruit onto the lined baking tray. Now the fun bit! Using two forks, pull the jackfruit into strips so it looks shredded. Add a splash of water to the sauce in the pan and spoon it over the shredded jackfruit until coated. Place in the oven for 15 minutes until starting to crisp at the edges.

7 Spoon the jackfruit on top of tortillas, with any spare sauce, and add any extra toppings you might like. I like to top mine with chopped avocado, tomato, coleslaw, and some fresh cilantro. A spoonful of dairy-free crème fraîche and salsa is great, too.

DID YOU KNOW?

Cauliflower is well-named because it is actually a flower! It is part of the same family as broccoli and cabbage, and is really good for you.

 **MEDIUM**

WHAT YOU NEED:

¾ cup all-purpose flour

1 teaspoon jerk spice mix

½ teaspoon garlic powder

salt & black pepper

¾ cup oat milk

1 whole cauliflower, leaves removed, broken into large bite-size florets

½–1 teaspoon hot sauce, to taste (it's pretty hot!)

1 tablespoon maple syrup

1 teaspoon sunflower oil

HOT CAULI BITES

Serves 4
Takes 50 minutes

These cauli florets are dipped in a spiced batter and baked in the oven until golden. They're delicious dunked into dairy-free mayo, and I also like to add a spoonful of sweet chili sauce.

1 To make the batter, mix together the all-purpose flour, jerk spice mix, garlic powder, and oat milk in a large mixing bowl. Season with salt and pepper.

2 Preheat the oven to 375°F. Line a large baking tray with parchment paper.

3 Dip the cauliflower florets, one at a time, into the thick, spicy batter until coated all over. Let them drip a little over the bowl to remove any excess batter, then place them slightly spaced apart on the lined baking tray.

4 Bake for 20 minutes, turning once, until light golden all over and the batter sets.

5 Meanwhile, mix together the hot sauce, maple syrup, and sunflower oil.

6 Carefully remove the baking tray from the oven. Brush the hot sauce mixture over the cauliflower bites until coated, then put the tray back in the oven for another 20 minutes until golden. Place in a serving bowl then dive in, dunking them into a sweet chili mayo, if you like.

NO SPICE

WHAT YOU NEED:

For the base:

2 ⅓ cups
self-rising flour

½ teaspoon
baking powder

1 teaspoon
salt

2 tablespoons plain
vegan yogurt

1 tablespoon extra-virgin olive
oil, plus extra for drizzling

For the topping:

⅔ cup
tomato sauce

1 tablespoon
tomato paste

1 teaspoon dried
oregano

1 teaspoon garlic
powder

salt &
black pepper

1 handful of canned
or fresh pineapple
pieces

1 small red
onion, thinly
sliced into rings

1 red pepper,
deseeded
and sliced

⅔ cup vegan
mozzarella cheese,
torn into small pieces

1 handful of
basil leaves

MY TROPICAL PIZZA

Serves 4
Takes 45 minutes

I've used a quick, yeast-free pizza base that doesn't need time to rise, so it's perfect for lunchtime. Feel free to add your own favorite toppings.

1 First make the pizza dough, mixing together the flour, baking powder, and salt in a large bowl. Stir in the yogurt, olive oil, and ½ cup plus 1 tablespoon of water, first with a fork and then with your hands until it comes together into a slightly sticky ball of dough.

2 Place the dough onto a lightly floured work surface and knead for a few seconds until the dough is soft. Add another tablespoon of flour if it is too sticky. Shape your dough into a ball and leave it to sit for 15 minutes, covered.

3 Preheat the oven to 425°F. Sprinkle flour over a large baking tray.

4 Meanwhile, prepare the topping ingredients. To make the tomato sauce, mix together the tomato sauce, tomato paste, oregano, and garlic powder in a bowl, then season with salt and pepper to taste.

5 Roll out the dough on a lightly floured work surface the same size as the baking tray, keeping the edges slightly thicker than the middle.

6 Spread the tomato sauce over the dough, leaving a border around the edge.

7 Now have fun with the toppings! Scatter the pineapple pieces, red onion, red pepper, and mozzarella on top. Drizzle with a little olive oil and bake for 16–18 minutes until the base is cooked and the top is lovely, melted, and bubbling. Top with a few basil leaves, cut into wedges, and dig in.

DID YOU KNOW?
A pineapple can take nearly 2 years to grow!

DID YOU KNOW?
Even though quinoa (pronounced "keen-wah") is used as a grain, it is in fact a seed.

NO SPICE

WHAT YOU NEED:

1 cup multicolored quinoa, rinsed

1 ¾ cups vegetable stock

2 tablespoons olive oil

1 onion, chopped

4 green onions, thinly slice

3 garlic cloves, chopped

1 orange pepper, deseeded and chopped

1 pound cremini mushrooms, roughly chopped

12 cherry tomatoes, halved

1 teaspoon dried oregano

1 teaspoon all-purpose seasoning

salt & black pepper

1 handful of basil leaves, torn (optional)

MUSHROOM QUINOA SPECIAL

Serves 4
Takes 45 minutes

Who doesn't love a stir-fry? This mushoom one is a favorite and comes with super-healthy quinoa. Noodles or rice are good alternatives, too.

1 Put the quinoa in a saucepan and add the vegetable stock. Bring to a boil, then turn the heat down to low. Cover with a lid, and simmer for 12–15 minutes until the stock has been absorbed. Turn off the heat and leave the quinoa to sit until needed.

2 Meanwhile, heat the oil in a large frying pan over medium heat. Add the chopped onion and cook, stirring occasionally, for 5 minutes until softened.

3 Add most of the green onions, saving some of the green parts to scatter over the dish at the end. Stir in the chopped garlic, chopped orange pepper, and the chopped mushrooms. Stir-fry over a medium-high heat for 8 minutes until the mushrooms start to turn golden.

4 Add the halved cherry tomatoes, oregano, all-purpose seasoning, and 2 tablespoons of water and cook for another 5 minutes, stirring until the tomatoes start to break down. Season with salt and pepper to taste.

5 Spoon the quinoa into four serving bowls and top with the mushroom stir-fry. Finish with a scattering of basil leaves, if using, and the saved green bits of the green onions.

DIN DIN!

....

DID YOU KNOW?

Red peppers are ripe green peppers.
They taste sweeter as they ripen.

NO SPICE

WHAT YOU NEED:

2 tablespoons
olive oil

1 onion,
chopped

2 carrots, peeled
and cut into
small pieces

1 red pepper,
deseeded and cut
into small chunks

2 large garlic
cloves, finely
chopped

1 teaspoon
all-purpose
seasoning

1 teaspoon
dried thyme

13 ounces chilled or frozen
vegan ground "beef"

1 can chopped
tomatoes

1 tablespoon
ketchup

1 tablespoon
jerk marinade

1 cup
vegetable stock

1 ¾ pounds white
potatoes, peeled and
cut into large chunks

¾ pound sweet
potatoes, peeled and
cut into large chunks

3 ½ tablespoons
vegan butter,
cut into pieces

3–5 tablespoons
oat milk

salt &
black pepper

COTTAGE PIE

Serves 4
Takes 1 hour, 30 minutes

We all love cottage pie and this vegan version goes down really well with my family.

1 To make the ground "beef" part of the cottage pie, heat the olive oil in a saucepan over medium heat. Add the chopped onion, chopped carrots, and chopped red pepper and cook, stirring often, for 7 minutes until softened.

2 Add the garlic, all-purpose seasoning, and thyme and cook over for another minute.

3 Pour in the chopped tomatoes, ketchup, jerk marinade, and cook for 5 minutes, then add the stock and let simmer.

4 While the "beef" mixture is cooking, prepare the mashed potato topping. Put the white potatoes and sweet potatoes in a large pan and pour over enough cold water to cover. Bring to the boil over a high heat, then turn the heat down a little and cook the potatoes for 12–15 minutes until soft. Carefully drain the potatoes, asking an adult to help you, then put them back in the pan to dry off.

5 Add the vegan butter and 3 tablespoons oat milk and mash with a potato masher until smooth. Add more oat milk if needed, then season with salt and pepper to taste. Meanwhile, preheat the oven to 400°F.

6 Spoon the "beef" mixture into 4 individual ovenproof dishes or 1 large dish, then spoon the mash on top and spread out evenly with the back of a spoon. Rough up the mash with a fork and dot extra butter on top. Bake for 40 minutes, or until the top is golden. Serve with peas or your favorite green veg.

MEDIUM

WHAT YOU NEED:

1 tablespoon
vegetable oil

1 onion,
chopped

1 red pepper,
deseeded and
chopped

3 white potatoes,
about 1 pound, peeled
and cut into
bite-size chunks

3 carrots, peeled
and cubed

15 ounce can
chickpeas, drained

1 inch piece fresh
ginger, peeled
and finely grated

2 garlic cloves,
finely chopped

1 tablespoon fresh
thyme leaves

1 teaspoon
all-purpose seasoning

1–2 tablespoons
mild curry powder

1 vegetable
stock cube

1 tablespoon
tomato paste

salt &
black pepper

CHICKPEA CURRY

Serves 4
Takes 45 minutes

This is made with pantry-essential ingredients, so it is super easy. I also like to add sweet potatoes, but I've kept things simple here. Serve with rice, roti, or flatbread.

1 Heat the oil in a saucepan over medium heat. Add the chopped onion and chopped red pepper and cook, stirring occasionally, for 5 minutes until softened.

2 Stir in the potato chunks, cubed carrots, chickpeas, grated ginger, finely chopped garlic, thyme, all-purpose seasoning, and curry powder and cook for another 2 minutes.

3 Meanwhile, crumble the stock cube into 2 cups and 2 tablespoons of of just-boiled water until it dissolves. Stir in the tomato paste.

4 Pour the stock into the pan and give everything a good mix. When it starts to bubble, turn the heat down to medium-low, cover the pan with a lid, and simmer for 15–20 minutes until the vegetables are tender when pierced with a fork. Season with salt and pepper to taste. Serve sprinkled with a little extra fresh thyme, if you like, with rice, roti, or flatbread.

DID YOU KNOW?

Curry powder is made from a mix of spices, often turmeric, coriander, cumin, ginger, chili powder, and pepper. It can be mild, medium, or hot.

DID YOU KNOW?

Pasta can contain eggs, which is not vegan-friendly,
so do make sure you buy egg-free
lasagna sheets.

NO SPICE

WHAT YOU NEED:

2 tablespoons olive oil

1 onion, roughly chopped

1 red pepper, deseeded and chopped

4 garlic cloves, finely chopped

13 ounces chilled or frozen vegan ground "beef"

21 ounce jar tomato sauce

1 teaspoon ground cumin

1 teaspoon all-purpose seasoning

½ teaspoon ground allspice

1 teaspoon dried thyme

salt & black pepper

6 egg-free dried lasagna sheets

For the "cheesy" sauce:

3 ½ tablespoons vegan butter

⅓ cup all-purpose flour

2 cups and 2 tablespoons almond milk, warmed

¼ teaspoon ground nutmeg

3 tablespoons nutritional yeast flakes

MY SPECIAL LASAGNA

Serves 4
Takes 1 hour, 45 minutes

As you know I like spices, so it's no surprise that my recipe for lasagna contains a few just to liven things up a bit! Serve it with a salad or veg.

1 Prepare pasta according to package directions, and then set aside.

2 Heat the olive oil in a saucepan over medium heat. Add the chopped onion and cook, stirring, for 5 minutes until softened.

3 Add the chopped red pepper and finely chopped garlic and cook for another 5 minutes, stirring often, until softened.

4 Stir in the vegan ground "beef," tomato sauce, cumin, all-purpose seasoning, allspice, thyme, and ¼ cup of water and when the sauce starts to bubble, turn down the heat slightly. Partly cover the pan with a lid and cook for 20 minutes until reduced and thickened. Stir the sauce occasionally so it doesn't stick. Season with salt and pepper to taste.

5 Meanwhile, make the "cheesy" white sauce. Melt the vegan butter over low heat in a small pan. Using a small whisk, gradually stir in the flour. Cook, stirring, over low heat for 1 minute until it makes a light brown paste. Gradually, pour in the warm almond milk and cook for 5 minutes, stirring, until thickened. Stir in the nutmeg and nutritional yeast flakes.

6 Preheat the oven to 400°F.

7 Now it's time to put together the lasagna. You will need a deep ovenproof dish, about 7 x 11 inches. Spoon a third of the vegan ground "beef" mixture in the bottom of the dish. Top with a layer of lasagna noodles, breaking the sheets if needed so the "beef" is covered. Spoon another layer of "beef" on top followed by half the "cheesy" sauce. Now for another layer of lasagna sheets and the remaining "beef" mixture. Finish with a third layer of lasagna sheets and the rest of the "cheesy" sauce.

8 Bake the lasagna for 40–45 minutes until the top starts to bubble and turn golden. Now chow down!

MEDIUM

WHAT YOU NEED:

3 zucchini, ends trimmed and spiralized

2 tablespoons olive oil

4 green onions, thinly sliced

10 or so cherry tomatoes, halved

½ can sweetcorn, drained

10 ounces vegan "chicken" pieces

1 handful of sugar snap peas, halved diagonally

2 garlic cloves, finely chopped

½ teaspoon dried oregano

1 teaspoon all-purpose seasoning

½–1 teaspoon jerk spice mix

salt & black pepper

1 handful of fresh basil leaves (optional)

Vegan parmesan, grated, to serve (optional)

ZOODLENESE

Serves 4
Takes 20 minutes

Ask your mom or dad to get you a spiralizer—they're so fun and useful too; you can spiralize lots of different vegetables! Here, spiralized zucchini make a great stir-fry.

1 Put the spiralized zucchini in a bowl and set aside for later.

2 Heat the olive oil in a large wok or frying pan over medium-high heat. Add the thinly sliced green onions, halved cherry tomatoes, sweetcorn, vegan "chicken" pieces, and sugar snap peas and stir-fry for 3 minutes.

3 Add the garlic, oregano, all-purpose seasoning, jerk spice, and ½ cup of water and stir-fry for another minute.

4 Now add in the spiralized zucchini and stir-fry for 1 minute or until slightly softened—you want them to keep their shape and color. Season with salt and pepper to taste.

5 Spoon into bowls and top with basil leaves and vegan parmesan, if you like. Dig in!

DID YOU KNOW?
Zucchini, known as courgettes in
the UK, are about 95 percent water!

WHAT YOU NEED:

2 tablespoons
sunflower oil

1 onion,
chopped

1 red pepper,
deseeded and
chopped

1 green pepper,
deseeded and
chopped

4 garlic cloves,
finely chopped

1 teaspoon
ground allspice

½ teaspoon
turmeric powder

1 teaspoon all-purpose
seasoning

1 tablespoon fresh
thyme leaves

2 sweet potatoes,
about a pound,
peeled and cut into
bite-size chunks

1 pound butternut
squash, peeled,
deseeded, and cut
into bite-size chunks

¾ cup
vegetable stock

1 ¾ cups
coconut milk

1 Scotch bonnet,
left whole, or jalapeño
pepper, deseeded and
chopped (optional)

¼ can (4.75 oz)
callaloo or
spinach leaves

1 corn-on-the-cob,
kernals sliced off,
or 1 cup canned
sweetcorn

salt & black
pepper

ITAL RUNDOWN

Serves 4
Takes 45 minutes

Traditionally, "Ital" food means one-pot cooking in Jamaica and other parts of the Caribbean. This veggie stew is based on a typical dish and also includes coconut milk.

1 Heat the oil in a saucepan over medium heat. Add the chopped onion and cook, stirring occasionally, for 5 minutes until softened.

2 Add the chopped red pepper and green pepper and finely chopped garlic and cook for another 3 minutes, stirring often.

3 Stir in the allspice, turmeric, all-purpose seasoning, thyme, sweet potato, and butternut squash chunks.

4 Pour in the vegetable stock and coconut milk and add the whole Scotch bonnet or chopped pepper, if using. I like my rundown hot, but you don't need to use jalapeño pepper if it's not your thing! Bring to a boil, then turn the heat down to medium-low. Cover with a lid and simmer gently, stirring occasionally, for 10 minutes.

5 Add the callaloo or spinach and sweetcorn and cook for another 5–10 minutes until all the vegetables are tender. Take care that the Scotch bonnet doesn't burst when stirring or it will make everything very spicy! Season with salt and pepper, then eat up. I like to serve it with rice.

Take care...

Only use the Scotch bonnet pepper if you like lots of heat—it's very spicy! You could use a milder tasting pepper instead, like a jalapeño, or leave it out altogether. It's a good idea to wear rubber gloves when chopping up pepper, and make sure you don't touch your face after cutting it.

NO SPICE

WHAT YOU NEED:

1 tablespoon olive oil

1 onion, chopped

1 red pepper, deseeded and chopped

½ pound cremini mushrooms, sliced

2 garlic cloves, finely chopped

2 cups lentils, rinsed

1 teaspoon ground allspice

1 teaspoon all-purpose seasoning

1 tablespoon fresh thyme leaves

2 bay leaves

14 ounce can chopped tomatoes

2 tablespoons tomato paste

2 ½ cups vegetable stock

salt & black pepper

14 ounces dried egg-free spaghetti

vegan parmesan, grated, to serve

LENTIL BOLOGNESE

Serves 4
Takes 1 hour, 15 minutes

Who needs meat, when you have lentils! This is a favorite weekday meal in my family. Serve it with some green veggies.

1 Heat the olive oil in a saucepan over medium heat. Add the chopped onion and cook, stirring occasionally, for 5 minutes until softened.

2 Add the chopped red pepper, sliced mushrooms, and finely chopped garlic and cook for 10 minutes until softened.

3 Stir in the lentils, allspice, all-purpose seasoning, thyme, bay leaves, chopped tomatoes, tomato paste, and stock. When the sauce starts to bubble, turn the heat down a little. Partly cover the pan with a lid and simmer for 40 minutes, stirring occasionally, until the lentils are cooked. Season with salt and pepper to taste.

4 About 15 minutes before the bolognese sauce is ready, bring a large pan of salted water to a boil. Add the pasta, stir, and cook for 10–12 minutes until just tender. Carefully drain the pasta, asking an adult to help you, and divide between four shallow bowls or plates. Spoon the sauce on top and serve with a sprinkling of vegan parmesan.

DID YOU KNOW?

Lentils are nutritious and cheap to buy. Made up of over 25 percent protein, they make a good meat substitute.

DID YOU KNOW?

Eating vegetables every day is good for your health. Make sure
you eat a range of different colored ones.

 **MEDIUM**

WHAT YOU NEED:

14 ounce can
chopped
tomatoes

1 tablespoon olive
oil, plus extra
for drizzling

2 garlic cloves,
finely chopped

1 onion,
chopped

1 red pepper,
deseeded and
thickly sliced

1 teaspoon
dried thyme

1 teaspoon
all-purpose
seasoning

1 teaspoon
jerk marinade

1 sweet potato,
peeled, cut in half
and thinly sliced into
¼ inch chunks

1 yellow pepper,
deseeded and
thickly sliced

1 orange pepper,
deseeded and
cut into chunks

½ pound butternut
squash, peeled,
deseeded, and
thinly sliced into
¼ inch chunks

2 zucchini,
sliced

salt & black
pepper

McQUEEN RATATOUILLE

Serves 4
Takes 1 hour, 20 minutes

This is a step up from your regular ratatouille! The veggies are roasted in a great-tasting, spicy red pepper and tomato sauce.

1 Put the chopped tomatoes, oil, garlic, onion, red pepper, thyme, all-purpose seasoning, and jerk marinade in a blender and blend until almost smooth. Season with salt and pepper to taste and set aside.

2 Preheat the oven to 400°F.

3 Now's the time to get layering! Arrange an even layer of sweet potatoes in the bottom of a large ovenproof dish, about 9 x 13 inches, and top with a third of the tomato sauce. Next add a layer of yellow and orange peppers and another third of the tomato sauce. Top with the butternut squash and the remaining tomato sauce. Finish with a layer of zucchini. Drizzle some more olive oil on top and season with salt and pepper to taste.

4 Cover the dish with foil and bake for 45 minutes. Carefully take off the foil and cook for another 10 minutes or until the vegetables are tender and starting to turn golden on top. Serve with bread for dunking into the sauce.

MEDIUM

WHAT YOU NEED:

14 ounces egg-free fusilli

2 tablespoons olive oil

4 green onions, thinly sliced

1 yellow pepper, deseeded and cut into chunks

1 green pepper, deseeded and cut into chunks

1 red pepper, deseeded and cut into chunks

3 garlic cloves, finely chopped

1 teaspoon oregano

1 teaspoon all-purpose seasoning

1 teaspoon jerk marinade

1 cup dairy-free crème fraîche

4 ounces vegan mozzarella, thinly sliced

salt & black pepper

1 handful of fresh basil leaves (optional)

vegan cheddar cheese, coarsely grated, to serve

RASTA PASTA

Serves 4
Takes 30 minutes

This colorful pasta dish has a delicious creamy, cheesy sauce—and it's all dairy-free!

1 Cook the pasta in a large saucepan of boiling salted water following the instructions on the packet.

2 Meanwhile, heat the olive oil in a large, deep frying pan over medium heat. Add the sliced green onions and the chopped yellow, green, and red peppers and cook, stirring often, for 5 minutes until softened. Turn the heat down slightly if the vegetables start to turn brown. Stir in the finely chopped garlic, oregano, all-purpose seasoning, and jerk marinade and cook for another minute.

3 Turn the heat down to low. Spoon in the dairy-free crème fraîche and thinly sliced mozzarella and cook gently, stirring for 5 minutes until you have a creamy sauce.

4 Your pasta should be ready now. Carefully drain it, asking an adult to help you, and save ½ cup of the cooking water.

5 Stir the pasta cooking water into the creamy sauce, then season with salt and pepper to taste.

6 Add the cooked pasta and stir everything with a large spoon until the pasta is coated in the sauce. Now you're ready to serve. Top with a few basil leaves, if you like, and grated vegan cheddar for an extra cheesy hit.

DID YOU KNOW?

Butter beans, also known as lima beans, are named after their butter-like color and creamy texture.

SPICE ALERT

WHAT YOU NEED:

2 tablespoons olive oil

1 onion, chopped

4 green onions, chopped

3 garlic cloves, chopped

2 large carrots, quartered lengthways and chopped

¾ pound butternut squash, peeled, deseeded, and chopped

1 teaspoon all-purpose seasoning

1 teaspoon ground allspice

1 teaspoon dried thyme

1 teaspoon jerk marinade

2 14 ounce cans jackfruit, drained, pieces halved if large

15 ounce can butter beans, drained and rinsed

1 tablespoon browning or soy sauce

2 ½ cups vegetable stock

1 tablespoon ketchup

½ cup tomato sauce

1 Scotch bonnet pepper, left whole (optional)

salt & black pepper

BROWN JACKFRUIT STEW

Serves 4
Takes 1 hour

Brown stew is a typical dish eaten for dinner throughout the Caribbean. I've included jackfruit, vegetables, and butter beans in my version.

1 Heat the olive oil in a large saucepan over a medium heat. Add the chopped onion and cook, stirring occasionally, for 5 minutes until softened.

2 Add the chopped green onions, chopped garlic, chopped carrots, and butternut squash chunks and cook, stirring for another 5 minutes.

3 Stir in the all-purpose seasoning, allspice, and thyme followed by the jerk marinade, jackfruit, and butter beans.

4 Now mix in the browning or soy sauce, stock, ketchup, and tomato sauce. When the sauce starts to bubble, turn the heat down. Put the lid on and simmer for 25–30 minutes, stirring every so often, until the vegetables are cooked. Add the whole Scotch bonnet pepper halfway through cooking if you like spice, or you can leave it out! Take the lid off the stew if the sauce is too runny and you need to reduce the liquid.

5 When it's ready, season with salt and pepper and serve with some delicious plain rice or Rice 'n' Peas (see page 82).

Take care...
Only use the Scotch bonnet pepper if you like lots of heat—it's very spicy! You could use a milder tasting pepper instead, like a jalapeño, or leave it out altogether. It's a good idea to wear rubber gloves when chopping up pepper, and make sure you don't touch your face after cutting it.

NO SPICE

WHAT YOU NEED:

1 tablespoon olive oil

2 onions, thinly sliced

3 garlic cloves, finely chopped

1 teaspoon smoked paprika

1 teaspoon ground cumin

1 teaspoon all-purpose seasoning

2 teaspoons plain flour

1 ½ cups coconut drinking milk

7 ounces spinach leaves, stalks removed

3 sweet potatoes, peeled and thinly sliced

grated vegan cheddar cheese, enough to cover the top

salt & black pepper

SWEET POTATO & SPINACH BAKE

Serves 4
Takes 1 hour, 30 minutes

This one-dish meal makes a simple and easy family dinner. Serve with extra veggies on the side.

1 Preheat the oven to 400°F.

2 Heat the olive oil in a large, deep frying pan over medium heat. Add the thinly sliced onion and cook for 9 minutes, stirring often, until softened. Add the finely chopped garlic and cook for another minute.

3 Stir in the smoked paprika, cumin, all-purpose seasoning, and flour and cook, stirring, for 1 minute.

4 Pour in the coconut drinking milk, turn the heat down, and simmer, stirring, for 2–3 minutes until thickened slightly. Season with salt and pepper to taste.

5 Meanwhile, steam the spinach for 3 minutes until the leaves are tender. Mix the spinach into the coconut sauce.

6 Spoon a quarter of the sauce into a large ovenproof dish. Top with a layer of thinly sliced sweet potato. Spoon another layer of sauce and then more sweet potatoes. Repeat once more, finishing with a final layer of sauce, so you have 3 layers of potato and 4 layers of sauce. Cover the dish with foil and bake for 50 minutes until the sweet potatoes are tender.

7 Carefully remove the dish from the oven. Take off the foil and scatter the vegan cheese over the top, then return to the oven for another 10 minutes until the cheese has melted.

DID YOU KNOW?

Sweet potatoes are not actually potatoes! Potatoes come from the tubers of a plant, while sweet potatoes are root vegetables.

NO SPICE

WHAT YOU NEED:

2 tablespoons
olive oil, separated

1 teaspoon
all-purpose
seasoning

2 tablespoons
jerk marinade
or sauce

1 tablespoon
maple syrup

7 ounces smoked
tofu, cut into
16 x ½ inch cubes

1 large yellow
pepper, deseeded
and cut into
16 chunks

2 red onions,
halved and cut
into 16 small
wedges

1 large red pepper,
deseeded and
cut into 16 chunks

2 zucchini,
cut into
16 thick slices

salt &
black pepper

Lime wedges,
to serve

SIMPLE KEBABS

Serves 4
Takes 30 minutes, plus marinating

You can swap any of the vegetables for your own favorites, but a mix of colors looks best. These kebabs make great summer food, especially when cooked on the barbecue.

1 Soak 8 wooden kebab sticks in cold water for 30 minutes—this will stop them from burning when cooking the kebabs.

2 Meanwhile, mix together 1 tablespoon of the olive oil, the all-purpose seasoning, jerk marinade or sauce, and maple syrup in a shallow dish. Add the tofu to the dish, stir with a spoon until coated, then set aside for 30 minutes to let it soak up all the flavors of the marinade.

3 Put all the vegetables in a large mixing bowl. Pour over the remaining 1 tablespoon olive oil, season with salt and pepper, and mix everything together with your hands until the vegetables are coated in the seasoned oil.

4 Preheat the grill to high (you can also cook the kebabs on a griddle pan or barbecue).

5 Thread the vegetables and tofu onto the wooden kebab sticks. I used 2 pieces of each type.

6 Grill the kebabs for 10 minutes, turning them occasionally, until golden in places. Serve with lime wedges for squeezing over and your favorite dipping sauce. Rice, quinoa, or roti are good, too.

ON THE SIDE!

....

MILD

WHAT YOU NEED:

2 cups all-purpose flour

½ teaspoon sea salt

½ teaspoon all-purpose seasoning

1½ tablespoons mild curry powder

3 ½ tablespoons vegan butter, melted

2 tablespoons sunflower oil

MY ROTI

Makes 6
Takes 45 minutes

I love roti! It's such an easy bread to make. No yeast, no kneading… I also love to add a bit of curry powder to the dough, just to give another level of flavor.
of flavor.

1 Put the flour, salt, all-purpose seasoning, and curry powder into a mixing bowl and give it a mix.

2 Stir in the melted vegan butter and ½ cup of water and mix, first with a fork and then your hands and shape into a ball of dough.

3 Place the dough onto a lightly floured work surface and shape into a long rectangle. Slice the dough into 6 equally sized pieces and roll each one into a ball.

4 Take one of the pieces and roll it out thin and round with a rolling pin.

5 Make a vertical cut from the edge to the center. Spread 1 teaspoon of the oil over the top with your hands, or use the back of a spoon.

6 Roll the dough up into an ice cream-cone shape. Fold over the top and push it into the center of the cone, then do the same with the bottom.

7 Shape the dough into a ball again, then roll out into a round— it should be as flat as a quarter. Repeat steps 4-7 for each piece of remaining dough.

8 Heat a dry frying pan over high heat. When the pan is hot, carefully put the roti into the pan. Cook for 1½–2 minutes on each side until it bubbles up and turns golden in places. Wrap in foil to keep warm and repeat with the rest of the dough until you have made six roti.

DID YOU KNOW?

Cabbage has been grown in the world for over 6,000 years—longer than any other vegetable!

NO SPICE

WHAT YOU NEED:

4 ounces white cabbage, shredded

4 ounces red cabbage, shredded

1 large carrot, coarsely grated

½ small red onion, thinly sliced

1 small red pepper, deseeded and thinly sliced

½ cup vegan mayonnaise

Juice of ½ lemon

salt & black pepper

2 tablespoons freshly chopped cilantro (optional)

CRUNCHY COLORFUL COLESLAW

Serves 4
Takes 20 minutes

Packed with colorful, healthy vegetables, this crunchy coleslaw is a great side to vegan burgers, wraps, and pizza.

1 Using a sharp knife, thinly slice the white and red cabbage, or you could coarsely grate it. Put the cabbage, in a serving bowl.

2 Add the grated carrot, thinly sliced red onion, and thinly sliced red pepper to the bowl.

3 Add the vegan mayo and lemon juice and stir until everything is mixed together nicely. Season with salt and pepper and scatter over with cilantro, if using. It's now ready to serve or keep in the fridge for up to 2 days.

WHAT YOU NEED:

1 tablespoon sunflower oil

1 onion, chopped

3 garlic cloves, finely chopped

1 teaspoon dried thyme

½ teaspoon all-purpose seasoning

½ teaspoon ground allspice

2 ½ cups brown basmati rice, rinsed

15 ounce can tin red kidney beans, not drained

1 Scotch bonnet pepper, left whole (optional)

1 ¾ cups coconut milk

salt & black pepper

RICE 'N' PEAS

Serves 4
Takes 35 minutes

This is a traditional Jamaican rice dish, flavored with thyme and allspice, and my favorite Scotch bonnet pepper! The peas aren't peas at all, they're actually kidney beans.

1 Heat the oil in a saucepan over medium heat. Add the onion and cook, stirring occasionally, for 5 minutes until softened. Add the garlic and thyme and cook for another minute.

2 Stir in the rice, all-purpose seasoning, allspice, and red kidney beans with the liquid from the can. Add the Scotch bonnet pepper, if using, then pour in the coconut milk.

3 Pour in enough cold water to cover the rice by half an inch and bring to a boil. Turn the heat down to the lowest setting and cover the pan with a lid. Simmer gently for 20 minutes or until the rice is tender and the water and coconut milk have been absorbed.

4 Remove the Scotch bonnet pepper and season with salt and pepper to taste. Spoon into a serving bowl—you can scatter some fresh cilantro leaves on top to add a bit of extra color if you like.

Take care...
Only use the Scotch bonnet pepper if you like lots of heat—it's very spicy! You could use a milder tasting pepper instead, like a jalapeño, or leave it out altogether. It's a good idea to wear rubber gloves when chopping up pepper, and make sure you don't touch your face after cutting it.

DID YOU KNOW?

Rice is one of the most important crops grown
throughout the world, feeding billions of people everyday.

DID YOU KNOW?
Peri-peri is a mix of herbs, spices, and seasonings. It's also called piri-piri.

SPICE ALERT!

WHAT YOU NEED:

5 white baking potatoes, about 1 ⅔ pounds, skin left on and cut lengthways into thick wedges

½ teaspoon sea salt

1 teaspoon garlic powder

1 teaspoon peri-peri spice mix

2 tablespoons olive oil

salt & black pepper

PERI-PERI WEDGES

Serves 4
Takes 1 hour, plus soaking

If you love spices you'll love my potato wedges! But don't worry you can leave them out if you prefer—they still taste great! Serve as a side with vegan mayo or ketchup.

1 Put the potatoes in a large mixing bowl and pour over enough cold water to cover. Stir in ½ teaspoon of salt. Leave to soak for 30 minutes. Swish the potatoes around with your hands, then drain and pat dry with paper towel. Soaking the potatoes first helps your wedges to crisp up when roasted.

2 Preheat the oven to 400°F.

3 Meanwhile, mix together the garlic powder, peri-peri spice mix, and the olive oil in a large mixing bowl. Season with salt and pepper.

4 Add the potato wedges to the bowl and turn them with your hands to coat with oil.

5 Place the wedges onto a large baking tray and spread out evenly—you may need to use 2 trays. Roast for 45–50 minutes, carefully turning once, until golden brown. They're now ready to eat with your favorite sauce!

NO SPICE

WHAT YOU NEED:

1 uncooked beetroot, peeled and coarsely grated

2 celery sticks, thinly sliced

1 small cucumber, quartered lengthways, deseeded, and cut into small pieces

3 green onions, thinly sliced

For the dressing:

Juice of ½ lemon

Juice of 1 lime

1 tablespoon olive oil

salt & black pepper

ZINGY BEETROOT SALAD

Serves 4
Takes 20 minutes

A crunchy, colorful salad with a zingy citrus dressing. It's a good idea to wear rubber gloves when grating the beetroot; otherwise you'll get pink hands!

1 Put the coarsely grated beetroot, thinly sliced celery, chopped cucumber, and thinly sliced green onions in a serving bowl.

2 To make the dressing, using a fork or small whisk, mix together the lemon and lime juice with the olive oil. Season with salt and pepper to taste. Now it's ready to serve!

DID YOU KNOW?

Beetroot is a root vegetable, like carrots, parsnips, and yams, and because it grows underground, it absorbs nutrients from the soil.

YUMMY EVER AFTER!

TROPICAL FRUIT SALAD

WHAT YOU NEED:

1 small pineapple, skin and core removed and cut into small chunks

1 mango, peeled, pitted, and cut into small chunks

3 handfuls of strawberries, halved if large

2 kiwis, peeled and cut into small chunks

2 handfuls of red seedless grapes, halved if large

1 green-skinned apple, quartered, cored, and cut into small chunks

Juice of ½ lemon

Serves 4
Takes 20 minutes

I've chosen some of my favorite fruits here, but you can swap in your own. Papaya, lychees, dragon fruit, raspberries, blackberries, and melon are all delicious, too.

1 Using a sharp knife, cut the green leaves off the pineapple and stand it upright on a chopping board. Carefully cut away the skin, slicing from top to bottom. Cut the pineapple into ½ inch thick round slices and then cut each slice into quarters. Slice off the hard core in the middle and cut the fruit into bite-size chunks.

2 Slice the mango lengthways on either side of the large pit in the middle, cutting as close to the pit as possible. Make crisscross diagonal cuts in each half taking care not to cut through the skin. Take one half in your hand and gently push out the fruit, slice off the cubes, then repeat with the second half.

3 Prepare the rest of the fruit. Halve the strawberries, if large. Peel the kiwis and cut into chunks. Halve the grapes, if large. Quarter the apple, remove the core, then cut into chunks.

4 Now that the hard part is done, put all your tasty fruits into a serving bowl. Squeeze the juice from the lemon all over the fruit, mix together gently, and serve.

DID YOU KNOW?

Apples are one of the most popular fruits in the world and provide a wide range of health benefits. The lemon juice will stop the apple from turning brown after it has been sliced.

DID YOU KNOW?

Agar-agar is made from seaweed
and is a vegan alternative to gelatin, which is
made from animal bones. It helps the jelly to set.

MANGO & COCONUT JELLIES

WHAT YOU NEED:

For the coconut jelly:

1 ¾ cups coconut milk

2 tablespoons maple syrup

½ teaspoon agar-agar flakes

1 teaspoon vanilla extract

For the mango jelly:

1 cup canned mango purée

1 tablespoon maple syrup

½ teaspoon agar-agar flakes

Coconut chips, to decorate
(optional)

Serves 4
Takes 25 minutes, plus setting

These are so good—there's a layer of coconut jelly, topped with a second layer of mango jelly. A taste of sunshine!

1 To make the coconut jelly, put the coconut milk and 2 tablespoons of maple syrup in a small pan. Using a small whisk, whisk in ½ teaspoon of agar-agar flakes. Bring to a boil over medium-low heat without stirring. When the mixture just starts to bubble, turn the heat to low and simmer for 10 minutes, stirring often, until thickened slightly.

2 Carefully strain the coconut mixture through a small sieve into four small glasses to make an even layer, then chill in the fridge for 2–4 hours until the jelly sets.

3 To make the mango jelly, put the mango purée and 1 tablespoon of maple syrup in a small pan. Using a small whisk, whisk in ½ teaspoon of agar-agar flakes. Bring to a boil over a medium-low heat without stirring. When a mixture just starts to bubble, turn the heat down to low and simmer for 5 minutes, stirring often, until thickened slightly. Leave to cool.

4 Pour the mango mixture over the coconut jelly in the four small glasses. Put the glasses back in the fridge for another 1 hour to set. Decorate with coconut chips sprinkled over the top, if you like, just before serving.

PLUM & BLACKBERRY CRUMBLE

WHAT YOU NEED:

For the crumble topping:

1 ¼ cups all-purpose flour

6 tablespoons vegan butter, cut into bite-size pieces, chilled

8 tablespoons light soft brown sugar, separated

⅓ cup porridge oats, separated

For the fruit base:

8 purple plums, about 1 ½ pounds, halved, pitted, and chopped

½ pound blackberries

½ teaspoon ground nutmeg

1 tablespoon demerara sugar, for sprinkling

Serves 4
Takes 1 hour, 30 minutes

A favorite dessert for a cold day! Feel free to swap out the fruit for your own choice, depending on what's in season. Great with dairy-free custard, ice cream, or cream!

1 Preheat the oven to 350°F.

2 To make the crumble topping, put the flour in a mixing bowl with the vegan butter and rub with your fingertips to make a nice, coarse, crumbly mixture. Stir in 6 tablespoons each of the light brown sugar and the oats. Chill the mixture in the fridge while you make the fruit base.

3 Cut the plums in half around the middle, take out the pits, then chop the fruit.

4 Put one of the plums and a handful of blackberries, the nutmeg, and the rest of the light soft brown sugar into a blender and blend until smooth.

5 Pour the blended fruit mixture into a mixing bowl and stir in the rest of the plums and blackberries. Taste to make sure it's sweet enough and add a bit more sugar if the fruit is still too sour. Spoon the fruit mixture into four individual baking dishes or one large ovenproof dish.

6 Scatter the crumble on top of the fruit in an even layer and sprinkle over some demerara sugar. Bake for 45 minutes until nice and golden on top.

DID YOU KNOW?
Bananas are great for giving you
a burst of energy—that's
why athletes like
to eat them!

BANANA FRITTERS

WHAT YOU NEED:

4 ripe bananas, peeled
and mashed

¼ cup brown sugar

1 teaspoon vanilla extract

¼ teaspoon ground nutmeg

½ teaspoon ground cinnamon

A pinch of salt

4 tablespoons almond milk

1 cup plain flour

½ teaspoon baking powder

Coconut oil, for frying

Serves 12
Takes 25 minutes, plus resting

Everyone loves banana fritters—me included! And these ones come with a touch of cinnamon. I like to serve them with coconut yogurt, lots of fruit, and a drizzle of maple syrup.

1 Mash the bananas and brown sugar with a fork in a large mixing bowl.

2 Now stir in the vanilla, nutmeg, cinnamon, and salt with a wooden spoon. Mix in the almond milk.

3 Gradually mix in the flour and baking powder to make a thick batter. Leave to rest for 10 minutes.

3 Melt enough coconut oil to coat the bottom of a large frying pan over medium heat.

4 Add a large spoonful (about 3 tablespoons) of the batter to the pan for each fritter—you should be able to cook about 3 at a time. Cook the fritters for 1½–2 minutes on each side, using a spatula to turn them. Continue until you have made 12 fritters. Place on on paper towels and keep warm in a low oven.

5 Serve the fritters with coconut yogurt and your favorite fruit by the side and pour over maple syrup. And there you have Banana Fritters!

ROCKY ROAD

WHAT YOU NEED:

⅔ cup shelled pistachio nuts

½ cup whole blanched almonds

⅔ cup extra-virgin coconut oil

3 ½ ounces vegan plain chocolate, broken into pieces

⅓ cup vegan cocoa powder or cacao powder

4 tablespoons maple syrup

2 tablespoons plant-based milk

2 ounces dried mango, cut into small pieces

2 ½ ounces vegan marshmallows, halved if large

2 ⅔ ounces animal crackers or similar cookie broken into chunks

Makes 12
Takes 30 minutes

Packed with vegan marshmallows, crackers, dried mango, nuts, and dairy-free plain chocolate, this rocky road is the best!

1 Preheat the oven to 325°F. Line an 8 x 8 inch square baking dish with parchment paper.

2 Put the pistachios and almonds on a large baking tray and toast in the oven for 10–15 minutes, turning occasionally, until light golden brown. Remove from the oven and leave to cool.

3 Meanwhile, melt the coconut oil and plain chocolate in a small pan over low heat. Beat in the cocoa powder, then leave to cool slightly.

4 Mix together the maple syrup and plant-based milk in a mixing bowl. Using a whisk, slowly whisk in the melted chocolate mixture.

5 Roughly chop the roasted nuts, then mix them with the mango, marshmallows, and crackers in a large mixing bowl. Take out a handful of the mixture and save for later.

6 Add the chocolate mixture to the bowl of nuts, marshmallows, and crackers and mix together well, so all the pieces are coated. Spoon into the lined baking pan and level the top with the back of the spoon.

7 Sprinkle the reserved nut mixture over the top and press down lightly to help them stick. Chill for about 1 hour, or until firm. Cut into 12 pieces and enjoy!

STRAWBERRY COCONUT CHEESECAKE

Serves 8
Takes 30 minutes, plus chilling

This fruity cheesecake is sure to impress your friends and family. What's more, it's completely dairy-free!

1 Line the base of a 8-inch round, springform cake pan with parchment paper.

2 Crush the crackers with a rolling pin until they turn into fine crumbs. It's less messy if you put them in a small bag first!

3 Put the crushed crackers into a mixing bowl and stir in the melted vegan butter and cinnamon until combined.

4 Spoon the cracker mixture into the lined cake pan and spread out evenly, pressing it down with the back of a spoon to make an even base. Chill in the fridge for about 20 minutes to firm up while you make the topping.

5 Using an electric hand whisk, mix together the cream cheese, vanilla extract, coconut cream, and ⅔ cup of the powdered sugar in a large mixing bowl until light and creamy. Stir in the lemon zest.

6 When the base is firm, spoon the cream cheese mixture on top and spread out evenly. Place in the freezer for 2 hours or until firm.

7 To make the strawberry topping, using a blender, purée ¾ of the strawberries with the rest of the powdered sugar and a squeeze of lemon juice until smooth.

8 Take the cheesecake out of the freezer about 1 hour before serving, then carefully remove from the pan. Put the cheesecake on a serving plate and spoon the strawberry sauce on top, letting it drizzle down the sides. Decorate with the remaining strawberries and nectarine slices. Delicious!

WHAT YOU NEED:

2 ¼ cups graham crackers, crushed

7 tablespoons vegan butter, melted

½ teaspoon ground cinnamon

2 cups vegan cream cheese

2 teaspoons vanilla extract

6 fluid ounces coconut cream

¾ cup powdered sugar, sifted, and separated

Finely grated zest of 1 small unwaxed lemon

1 ⅔ cups strawberries, halved

Squeeze of lemon juice

1 nectarine, halved, pit removed, and sliced

CHERRY BROWNIES

WHAT YOU NEED:

2 tablespoons ground flaxseeds

1 cup self-rising flour

¾ cup ground almonds

½ cup cocoa powder

¼ teaspoon baking powder

¼ teaspoon salt

⅔ cup dried sour cherries, halved

4 ½ ounces vegan plain chocolate

5 ½ tablespoons vegan butter

1 cup and 2 tablespoons golden caster sugar (can use superfine white sugar if golden caster unavailable)

5 tablespoons plant-based milk

1 ½ teaspoons vanilla extract

Makes 12 squares
Takes 1 hour, 15 minutes

Super chocolatey with a fudgey middle—no one will believe these brownies are vegan! If you don't like cherries you can use raisins or dried mango instead.

1 Preheat the oven to 350°F. Grease the base of a 8 x 8 inch square baking pan and line with parchment paper.

2 Mix the ground flaxseeds with 6 tablespoons of water and set aside for about 20 minutes until they form a jellylike texture.

3 Meanwhile, put the flour, almonds, cocoa powder, baking powder, and salt in a mixing bowl and stir until combined. Mix in the dried cherries.

4 Melt the plain chocolate with the butter in a small pan over low heat. Pour into a separate mixing bowl and add the caster sugar.

5 Whisk together the melted chocolate mixture and caster sugar until the sugar dissolves. Stir in the plant-based milk, vanilla, and soaked flaxseeds until combined.

6 Using a wooden spoon, stir the chocolate mixture into the flour mixture. Spoon into the prepared baking pan and level the top with a spatula. Bake for 35–45 minutes until cooked and firm to the touch—it should still be a bit gooey in the middle.

7 Leave to cool in the pan, then cut into 12 squares and place on a wire rack.

HELPFUL MEASUREMENT CONVERSIONS

3 teaspoons (tsp) of liquid = 1 tablespoon

8 tablespoons (tbsp) of liquid = ½ cup

1 cup of liquid = 8 fluid ounces

4 cups of liquid = 1 quart

COOKERY WORDS

BAKE: to cook food, such as cakes, pies, and bread in an oven using dry heat. The outside of the food usually becomes golden brown.

ROAST: to cook food, such as vegetables, in an oven at a high temperature.

BOIL: to cook food in a saucepan of bubbling liquid, such as water or stock. When a liquid comes to a boil it bubbles and is very hot.

SIMMER: to cook food in liquid, such as stock or water, in a saucepan over low heat so the liquid is just below boiling point. The liquid can bubble gently.

STEW: to cook food slowly in a simmering liquid, such as stock or a sauce, in a covered casserole or saucepan.

FRY: to cook food in a frying pan in a small amount of oil or fat over direct heat.

DEEP FRY: to cook food submerged in hot oil in a deep saucepan or deep-fat fryer until crisp and golden.

SAUTÉ: to fry food quickly in a small amount of oil or fat over direct high heat, usually in a sauté pan (straight-sided frying pan).

DRY FRY: to fry food in a frying pan without oil or fat.

STIR-FRY: to fry food quickly over high heat in a little hot oil or fat in a wok or frying pan.

DICE: to cut food into small cubes.

CHOP: to cut food into small pieces.

PEEL: to remove the rind or skin from a fruit or vegetable using your hands, a small knife, or a vegetable peeler.

GRATE: to rub food against a grater into shreds, fine slices, or powder.

BLEND: to mix ingredients together into a liquid or smooth mixture using a food processor or blender.

KNEAD: to use your hands to massage or work ingredients together, such as bread dough, until it is elastic and smooth.

Thank you for cooking, hope you enjoyed...

NOW YOU'RE A CHEF!

Remember to share your amazing pictures and don't forget to tag me on social media. The kitchen is now your science lab—try experimenting with your own recipes, dishes, and flavor combinations.

Always try to stay humble, be yourself, work hard, and remember: your flaws make you unique.

Love, Omari

• •

FACEBOOK
Omari McQueen

INSTAGRAM
@omarimcqueen

TWITTER
@OmariMcQueen

TikTok
@omarimcqueen

SNAPCHAT
omari_mcqueen

YOUTUBE
The Mari Maker Show

Stay safe! Please remember the golden rules of online life:
- Think about waiting until you're 13 to use social media.
- Keep your location and personal information private.
- Be smart—don't agree to meet face-to-face with an online friend, or send them photos of yourself, until you've spoken to an adult you trust.
- Report anything abusive or that makes you feel uncomfortable to a trusted adult.
- Remember your digital footprint—everything you post online is permanent.

• •

INDEX